SPORTS GREAT HERSCHEL WALKER

— Sports Great Books —

Sports Great Roger Clemens
ISBN 0-89490-284-9

Sports Great John Elway
ISBN 0-89490-282-2

Sports Great Bo Jackson
ISBN 0-89490-281-4

Sports Great Magic Johnson
ISBN 0-89490-160-5

Sports Great Darryl Strawberry
ISBN 0-89490-291-1

Sports Great Herschel Walker
ISBN 0-89490-207-5

SPORTS GREAT HERSCHEL WALKER

Jim Benagh

— Sports Great Books —

ENSLOW PUBLISHERS, INC.
Bloy St. & Ramsey Ave.   P.O. Box 38
Box 777   Aldershot
Hillside, N.J. 07205   Hants GU12 6BP
U.S.A.   U.K.

Library of Congress Cataloging-in-Publication Data:

Benagh, Jim, 1937
    Sports Great Herschel Walker / by Jim Benagh.
        p. cm. — (Sports great books)
    Summary: Tells the life story of football running back
Herschel Walker, from his youth in the South up through his years
with the Minnesota Vikings.
    ISBN 0-89490-207-5
    1. Walker, Herschel — Juvenile literature. 2. Football players —
United States — Biography — Juvenile literature. 3. Running
backs (Football) — Juvenile literature. 4. Minnesota Vikings
(Football team) — Juvenile literature. [1. Walker, Herschel. 2.
Football players. 3. Afro-Americans — Biography.] I. Title. II.
Series.
GV6939.W32B46   1990
796.332'092 — dc20
[B]   89-28385
92   CIP
                                                          AC

Printed in the United States of America

10 9 8 7 6 5 4 3 2

Illustration Credits: Dallas Cowboys Weekly, pp. 54, 57; Will Hart, pp. 11, 17, 23, 42, 44, 47, 50; © 1989 Rick A. Kolodziej, pp. 10, 58; University of Georgia, pp. 21, 27, 32, 35; University of Georgia, Wingate Downs, p. 31; University of Georgia, Richard Fowlkes, p. 8; University of Georgia, Tim Gentry, pp. 14, 18.

Cover Photo: © 1989 Rick A. Kolodziej

Contents

Chapter 1

The date was September 6, 1980. Almost 95,000 football fans jammed Neyland Stadium in Knoxville, Tennessee, to watch the opening game of the season between the University of Tennessee Volunteers and the University of Georgia Bulldogs. The hometown fans were happy as their team got off to a fast start. Tennessee led, 9-0, late in the second quarter. Yet, somehow, something was wrong. Where was Herschel Walker, the Georgia freshman running back whom everyone was talking about? Why wasn't he playing?

Only the year before, Walker had been called the best high school running back in the entire nation. Numerous colleges had offered him scholarships. When he chose Georgia, it was expected that he would become an instant star.

However, in fall training, Walker had not lived up to his promise. When the season opened against Tennessee, two other running backs were ahead of him in the lineup. They were Donnie McMickens and Carnie Norris. Had all the college scouts been wrong about Walker? What was the real story about the big, fast star from Wrightsville, Georgia?

The first half of the game was sloppy, with fumbles by both teams. Georgia's attack seemed to sputter and stall whenever it got the ball. Finally, with less than six minutes left in the half, Georgia Coach Vince Dooley decided to use his big freshman running back.

With the ball on the Georgia 20-yard line, quarterback Buck Belue called Herschel's number in the huddle. Number

With his big reputation, pressure was on Herschel in his first college game.

34 took the handoff and rammed into the line for a gain of two yards. It was his first carry in college. Over the next three years, Herschel would carry the ball more than a thousand times.

Three plays later, Walker caught a screen pass from Belue and gained nine yards. Moments later, he took another pass, but there was a clipping penalty, which meant that one of the Georgia players blocked an opponent illegally from behind. Belue fumbled. Walker fell on the ball to keep possession for Georgia, but once again the Bulldogs' attack was stopped.

At times, the Georgia team actually moved backward. Just before the half ended, the Bulldogs began to move the ball. But, on the Tennessee 47, Belue found himself trapped by the Volunteers. He scrambled around trying to evade tacklers, but they ran him down for a 19-yard loss. An offside penalty lost five more yards. In two plays, Georgia had lost 24 yards, and the Bulldogs now needed 34 yards, not ten, for a first down.

In the third quarter Tennessee got another touchdown to make the score 15-0. At that point, Georgia looked terrible. The offense had fumbled four times, and the team had been penalized five times. The Bulldogs needed some breaks.

Late in the third quarter, Georgia was forced to punt again. Georgia boomed a sky-high punt that Tennessee took on its 27. But a stiff tackle sent the ball flying and squiggling downfield with both teams in pursuit. It wound up going outside of the Tennessee end zone for a Georgia safety, making the score Tennessee 15, Georgia 2.

After a safety, the team that scores gets the ball. So Georgia began a march, and the Bulldogs started to click. The team turned to Herschel. He gained four yards, then five, and then Belue picked up the first down on a quarterback sneak. Next, Belue passed to the Tennessee 18-yard line.

It was Herschel's turn again. The teams lined up, the ball

was snapped, and Walker took the handoff in high gear. He hit the line like a bulldozer, knocked over a linebacker, and cut between two defensive backs. He made it into the end zone, his first college touchdown — and the first of many. Georgia made the extra point and was behind only 15-9.

Tennessee was starting to feel the pressure, and fumbled after a couple of plays. Georgia recovered the ball. The

When Herschel went to the Vikings in 1989, it was a big story.

fired-up Bulldogs of Georgia sprang to the attack. Belue passed for eight yards, but the next play gained just one. It was Herschel's turn again. He went storming into the line for a first down on Tennessee's 23-yard line. Belue ran for nine yards, but on the next play Walker was stopped. Belue gave him another chance and this time he picked up a first down to the 8-yard line.

Before long, people began associating Herschel with college football's biggest prize, the Heisman Trophy.

After a Georgia penalty, Belue turned to his freshman again. First Herschel plunged for four yards. Then he took a handoff, raced left, cut right, and was into the Tennessee end zone before the Volunteers came to their senses. Herschel was too much, looking like the runner the University of Georgia and many others felt he could be. With the extra point, Georgia went ahead, 16–15.

The game was far from over, with more than a quarter to play. It was tough for both teams. The night was hot, and both teams got tired.

But Herschel still had energy. In fact, Herschel finished the evening with 84 yards in 24 carries as Georgia held on to win, 16–15. That wasn't a bad start for a freshman who played for only about half the game. In fact, it was good enough to earn him the Southeast Back of the Week honors from both The Associated Press and United Press International. More importantly, the outstanding college career of Herschel Junior Walker had begun.

Chapter 2

Herschel Junior Walker was born on March 3, 1962, near a small town called Wrightsville, Georgia.

The name Herschel is not uncommon in the state. From 1853 to 1857, a man named Herschel V. Johnson was governor of the state. The local football stadium was named after Herschel Lovett, a local banker. But the new Walker baby was named after his grandfather.

The Walker family was poor. Herschel's father, Willis, and his mother, Christine, met when they were teenagers picking cotton. They were married when they were sixteen years old. Herschel was the fifth of seven children. The others were named Willis, Jr., Renneth, Sharon, and Veronica. After Herschel came Lorenzo and Carol.

Herschel's parents worked for a farmer named Rex Jackson. Willis earned $25 a week doing various chores and driving farm machinery. Christine earned $10 a week cleaning the Jackson house. As a bonus, every Christmas, Mr. Jackson gave the Walkers $100 in cash and a 200-pound hog. Mr. Jackson liked the Walker family. He said, "Willis worked hard and faithfully for me for 16 years. The Walkers are a very special family. They don't drink, they don't stay out all night."

The Walkers lived a quiet life. Partly it was due to their community. People often said that Wrightsville was a town "five miles from nowhere." The population was only 2,500, most of them farm workers. People who wanted to go bowling or see a new movie had to drive 20 miles to towns called

For a future star, there were humble beginnings.

14

Swainsboro and Sandersville. Like most towns in rural Georgia at the time, Wrightsville was segregated, meaning it was divided into white areas and black areas. Two thirds of the people were white, the rest were black. Most of the young black people wanted to get away to find better opportunities. They dreamed of going to college and then moving on to live in bigger cities in Georgia such as Columbus, Macon, or Atlanta.

However, to rise in the world or get into a good college, many young African Americans became athletes. Years ago, some outstanding black Georgians rose to fame through athletics. Jackie Robinson, who became the first black man to play in major league baseball, was born in Cairo, Georgia. Jim Brown, who became the greatest running back in professional football history, was born on St. Simon's Island, off Georgia's coast. In years to come, Herschel Walker would be compared with Jim Brown.

The Walker family was deeply religious. Going to church on Sunday was a weekly event for everyone. The children spent their other time going to school, or working on the farm doing odd jobs. They kept out of mischief. To this day, Herschel does not drink or smoke.

Except for Herschel, all of the Walker children enjoyed sports. Mostly they liked to race against each other. But Herschel didn't care that much about sports. Physically, Herschel wasn't very developed. When he got into a scrape with another boy, he usually lost. Little Bo, as he was called, was a tubby youngster. He was particularly envious of his sister, Veronica, who was a little more than a year older and very fast. In a foot race, she left him far behind.

If Herschel felt close to anyone in his family, however, it was to Veronica and his mother. Yet, much of the time Herschel liked to be alone. He was something of a dreamer.

He tried never to bother anybody. He wanted to be independent. When he got sick, he would hesitate a long time before telling his mother.

At the age of six, Herschel began school. Those were happy years for him. He loved school. He couldn't wait to go to class to learn. He just liked to listen. He seldom spoke in school, but he did learn.

One thing he liked was poetry. He would wander off to a hillside and look out over the fields and trees. He tried to put his thoughts down in rhyme, because he hoped that some day he would become a writer. His poems weren't fancy, but they expressed what was in his heart and mind.

As he grew older, Herschel saw how much fun his brothers and sisters were having with sports. His older brothers — Willis, Jr., and Renneth — played football on the Johnson County High School team. And, if Veronica always beat him in a foot race, there was a good reason. Herschel didn't know then that his sister was one of the fastest girls in his area. One day she would earn a track scholarship to the University of Georgia. Still, other kids his age also beat him at running. One childhood friend remembered Herschel as "the slowest kid in our class."

When Herschel was 12 years old, he suddenly grew tired of losing. In his heart, he knew he could do better, but he just didn't know how to go about it. One day, very shyly, he approached a man named Tom Jordan, who coached the Johnson County High School track and field team. Jordan was also the grade-school physical education teacher.

Herschel asked politely: "Coach Jordan, how can I get to be big and strong?"

Tom Jordan smiled down at the pudgy youngster. He replied: "Do pushups. Do situps. Run sprints."

Herschel knew it was good advice. He began his own

It took time and hard work for Herschel to build up the marvelous physique that made him a superstar athlete.

training program. Every day, before and after school, before and after studies, before and after chores, he would do the pushups, the situps, and the sprints. He enjoyed the workouts.

Slowly but steadily he began to put muscles on his arms, his legs, and his shoulders. Before the year was over, he could do 300 pushups, or 300 situps, without stopping. Then he

Beating his sister, Veronica, in a footrace was one of Herschel's early goals.

would run as fast as he could for a few yards. He would ease up, rest for a moment or two, and begin running again.

However, some of Herschel's other habits were not very good for a young athlete. For example, he never slept much. Four, or perhaps five, hours a night were all he needed. Even today, he sleeps only a few hours a night. This is not because he doesn't get to bed on time. As an adult, someone asked Herschel what would happen if he got to bed by 10 o'clock in the evening. He answered, "In that case, I'd probably wake up at two or three o'clock in the morning."

Herschel's eating habits were also not the best, either. He would gulp down a lot of hamburgers, followed by a few candy bars.

Yet, in spite of his growing body, Herschel still could not beat his sister in a race. He tried hard, but she was always a little faster. Then, when Herschel was sixteen years old and a sophomore in high school, that changed.

One day Veronica challenged Herschel to race against her over the uphill course that was their track. They started out even, but Veronica never had a chance. Herschel beat her easily. They ran again, and Herschel won again — and again.

Veronica was crushed. She cried most of the night. She talked about quitting track. Her mother, as usual, said all the right things. Mrs. Walker pointed out that Herschel was now a big and powerful young man. Sooner or later he was bound to beat her. But Veronica was still fast enough to defeat most of the girls her own age, and probably a lot of boys as well.

Once he beat Veronica, Herschel wanted to find out just how fast he could run. He tried to beat a pet horse. His mother laughed. She said, "Herschel, you can't outrun a horse." And he couldn't.

Chapter 3

By the time Herschel Walker was sixteen years old, the fortunes of the family had changed. Everything was different — and better.

Dad, Mom, and the family left the Jackson farm and got better jobs. Mr. Walker worked in a mill that turned white clay into chalk. Mrs. Walker worked in a factory that made trousers.

Like all normal kids, the Walker boys often rough-housed with each other. They weren't mad, just playful. If things got out of hand, Mrs. Walker put her foot down firmly. When they weren't wrestling, they found other activities. They tried high jumping. They talked about jumping over their father's automobile. Willis Walker quickly put a stop to that. "You fool kids, that's my car! You'll get hurt. I've got no money to pay for hospitals."

However, Mr. Walker did have an adventurous streak. With a few spare dollars, he bought his sons a motorcycle. One day, Herschel almost ended up in the hospital after an accident with the bike. He was riding on a dirt road when the bike hit a rock and skidded. Herschel went flying over the handles and hit the ground with a crash. When he got up there was a bloody scrape on his forehead. Mrs. Walker made sure there would be no more motorcycles.

Herschel continued to grow, putting weight and muscles on his body. There was power in his legs, his arms, and his shoulders. And he could run like a rabbit.

Herschel got bigger and bigger. Hard work was his secret.

A new head football coach had come to Johnson County High School, a bright young man named Gary Phillips. Coach Phillips took one look at Herschel and realized that the youngster could become a star. He was a lot bigger and stronger than most of the high school players in that area. Tom Jordan, who also served as assistant football coach, agreed with Phillips. "That youngster will surprise you," Jordan said, "I know he always surprises me."

Johnson County High opened its season against Laurens County High. Herschel scored one touchdown on a 3-yard run. It was his only score of the day. He did carry the ball on other occasions. In eleven carries, he gained a total of 68 yards, including a run of 24 yards.

But it was on defense, as a linebacker, that Herschel really starred. He recovered two fumbles, made five solo tackles, and helped out on ten other tackles. Johnson County won, 26-0.

During the first few games, Johnson County used one trick that made the crowds laugh. Instead of ordinary jerseys, the running backs wore raggy T-shirts that tore apart as soon as a tackler pulled on them. When Johnson County wore white T-shirts, the numbers were painted on the back with black shoe polish. When blue T-shirts were used, the numbers were painted on with white shoe polish. The tearaway T-shirts didn't last very long. Other coaches began to complain and the idea was dropped.

Like all young players, Herschel made mistakes on the field. Coach Phillips did not know his young star as well as Coach Jordan did, and the two would decide together on how to correct Herschel's mistakes. "He doesn't like to be yelled at," Jordan told the head coach. "Just talk to him calmly. Herschel will get the message."

That was exactly what happened. Phillips would point out

a play when Herschel was out of position. The lad would reply: "Yes, sir. I know I didn't do it right that time. It won't happen again." And that was all there was to it.

Coach Phillips was not so easy on his players all the time, not even with Herschel. At times he thought they were too lackadaisical, too lazy. He would bark out: "Okay, you there! Let's have twenty pushups!"

For the young athlete who wants to become a pro star, the seeds of hard work have to be planted early.

Herschel, of course, never considered the pushups as a punishment. He would smile and ask, "How many?" Herschel could do the twenty or more, even one-handed.

Then, when the coach would ask him if he knew what he did wrong, Herschel would reply, usually in a polite and soft voice, "Yes, sir."

Johnson County High didn't win all their games when Walker was the star. In fact, one season, the team lost three games in a row. Herschel always managed to gain good yardage, though, and to do his share. The plays weren't tricky or difficult. For the most part, they were sweeps around right or left end, or a straight run into the line for a couple of yards and the first down. On end sweeps, Herschel often outran the defense so that he could "turn the corner." And when the linebackers caught up with him, he could usually drag them ahead for an extra yard or two.

He didn't just concentrate on athletics, either. Most of all, to him school was a place to learn. As a student he was very good. He was president of the Beta club, a school honor group. He would later graduate first in his senior class of 108 students. He had a 93 average. Such an academic showing would bring him scholarship offers from several Ivy League colleges.

He was never the kind to boast of his achievements on or off the field. Although he was one of the most popular students at Johnson County High, he did not seem to have very many dates, until his senior year. Then he would joke about girls with his coaches. He would show them a picture of a girl. In his somewhat squeaky voice, he would ask innocently, "Tell me, what do you think of my wife?"

Both coaches would laugh and go along with the joke. "Not bad," they would answer. "But when did you get married?"

Herschel's senior year was almost unbelievable. He gained a total of 3,167 yards. Coach Phillips said: "I think Herschel could have gained 5,000. But he seemed a little tired sometimes. Don't forget. He played offense and defense." Indeed! He finished that season in third place on the team for the most tackles made.

The college scouts had been watching Herschel closely for two years. Now they came swarming around in earnest. The recruiters came by plane, by car, and even by helicopter. But they had to be careful how they talked to the young star. To offer him money would have been illegal. They did find out that he was interested in becoming an agent for the Federal Bureau of Investigation. Once the recruiters learned that, Herschel began getting mailbags full of literature on criminal justice from universities trying to win his attention.

The scouts looked at Herschel's powerful body and wondered if he practiced lifting weights. Actually, he never did. Only once did he give it a try. The high school had purchased some barbells, and Herschel was curious about how heavy a load he could lift. He decided to try 250 pounds. He stepped up to the weight, raised it easily, pushed it up and down a few times, and set it down. "Coach," he said, "250 pounds isn't heavy."

Some recruiters did make some illegal offers. They would hint at the benefits he might get if he attended their schools. He was promised cars, jobs, and money for his family and himself.

Herschel wasn't about to listen, though. There were other considerations. For example, he was more interested in what kind of offense the college used. He would ask his own coaches and not listen solely to the recruiters.

When the University of Alabama was discussed, Herschel already knew that school ran from a "wishbone" attack. In a wishbone formation, three backs line up behind the quarterback. The backs start from a three-point stance, formed by one hand as well as two feet touching the field. Herschel knew he ran better when he started standing up, and therefore, he ruled out the University of Alabama.

Herschel also knew that Florida State and the University of Miami threw a lot of passes. That meant he would not get to run as much if he went there. "I'd rather go to a school where they run the ball," he would say.

Scholarship offers were coming in from everywhere. Florida State in the South, Southern California in the West — from every direction!

And there were worries by some recruiters that some school "got" to Herschel, especially when he began driving a $9,000 Pontiac Trans Am. But his father insisted the car was a graduation present. Willis Walker had worked double shifts on his factory job. He had taken out a bank loan. "Look at the bank records," Mr. Walker said. "We're not asking anybody for anything. Herschel won't take anything except from his own family."

The recruiters' calls seemed to never end. They did cease for a while, though, when Willis Walker ripped the telephone cord off the relay switch.

As spring of 1980 got nearer, Herschel knew he would have to make a decision soon on where to attend college. Sometimes he and his mother would play games, like flipping a coin to decide, or pulling slips of paper out of a hat with schools written on them. But Herschel finally made up his own mind. His decision: the University of Georgia.

There were not many people present when Herschel Walker signed the letter of intent to Georgia. There were members of his family, some local sportswriter friends, Coach

Phillips, Coach Jordan, and some members of the Georgia coaching staff.

When Georgia Coach Vince Dooley got the word, he said: "No, I didn't do a hand flip about Walker coming here." Then he smiled and added, "But that's only because I don't know how to do a hand flip."

Then, more seriously, the coach explained: "I know the boy is strong and fast. But he played only Class A high school football. The schools in Class A are small, most of the players are small. I don't expect Walker to help us a whole lot next season." Coach Dooley was in for a big surprise.

High school was over. It was time for Herschel to put on a new uniform, that of the University of Georgia.

Chapter 4

High school football had made Herschel a hero in Wrightsville. After he played his last game for Johnson County High, people all over the state of Georgia knew about him. Everyone said good things about him, that he was an excellent student, a leader, a future college football star, polite, and considerate. His future looked bright. But the spring of 1980 brought trouble to Wrightsville — and to Herschel.

It was a time of racial unrest all across America. African Americans were demanding their civil rights. They wanted jobs that paid good wages. They wanted an end to discrimination. There were protest marches and there was violence between black and white people. On one occasion in Wrightsville, Georgia, two young boys were beaten up. Later, four black youths were arrested and accused of doing it. Two boys who were accused had played on the high school basketball team with Herschel. Wrightsville seemed ready to explode. The governor of Georgia sent 200 state troopers into the town to keep order.

Perhaps the best known person in Wrightsville was a high

28

school senior named Herschel Walker. If he had been part of the protests and the violence, the news would have been printed in every paper in the state. But he chose to stay removed from the problems. He simply said: "I don't believe in black and white. I believe in right and wrong."

Many black people in the area were angry with Herschel. Other teenagers called him "honky-lover" and other names. They pointed out that many of his friends were white. That was true. Herschel was popular and easy going, and he, therefore, was liked by both black and white people. But now he was being forced to choose sides.

Herschel had often played tennis with a white girl. They were just friends, nothing more. Now, however, public opinion was against any sort of friendship between blacks and whites. The girl's parents called Herschel's parents. He had to stop playing tennis with her.

Many of the cheers he had heard on the playing field were now jeers. Black people threatened Herschel because he wouldn't join the protest marches. White people threatened him simply because he was black. Herschel was deeply hurt. He began to distrust everyone, except for his family and closest friends.

Among those he could talk to about his feelings were his high school coaches, Gary Phillips and Tom Jordan. Herschel told Phillips he wanted to forget about football and college. Instead, he was thinking about going into the Marine Corps. Jordan and Phillips advised him not to give up football. Herschel was going to college, and that was final. They promised to help him in any way they could. Herschel calmed down, but he stayed in his room much of the time. He often wrote poetry when he was by himself, and he had written about "time to move on."

For Herschel the end of the summer was a blessing. It was

time to move on — to college, at the University of Georgia, and back to football, where people judged him by what he did on the field.

His vacation was over, and summer football at the university in Athens, Georgia, was about to begin. Early one morning, Herschel awoke before sunrise. He packed the car with his belongings and drove away from home. He did not even wake up his family to bid them goodbye.

It did not take Herschel long to find that big time college football was a lot different from the smaller high schools he had been playing against. In the first contact scrimmage, Herschel took a handoff from the quarterback and dove into the line. There he was met by the nose guard, a giant named Eddie (Meat Cleaver) Weaver. Meat Cleaver stood six feet tall and weighed 270 pounds. They crashed into each other like a couple of runaway tractors. Herschel was wobbly when he got to his feet.

The play was tried again. Once more Herschel boomed into Weaver. This time, he spun off and managed to lunge ahead. But after that he fumbled. Then he struggled as he tried to pick his way through holes in the line. Later, he told a reporter: "I've never been hit harder in my life. He got me up high, just under the shoulder pads."

Head Coach Vince Dooley had said that he didn't expect too much from the freshman Walker that fall. Besides, the coach didn't think any freshman should be a starter when there were two more experienced running backs on the team. For those reasons, Herschel did not make the starting lineup for the opening game with Tennessee. However, after the next game of the season, there was no doubt that Georgia's number one running back was Herschel Junior Walker.

Game two was against Texas A&M and it was the home opener for the Georgia Bulldogs. It promised to be a close game because both teams had to work hard to win their first games the week before.

But the game turned out to be a runaway for Georgia. Quarterback Buck Belue's passes were on target, and the new tailback, Herschel Walker, was running well—biting out chunks of yardage everytime he carried the ball. At the half, Georgia led, 28–0.

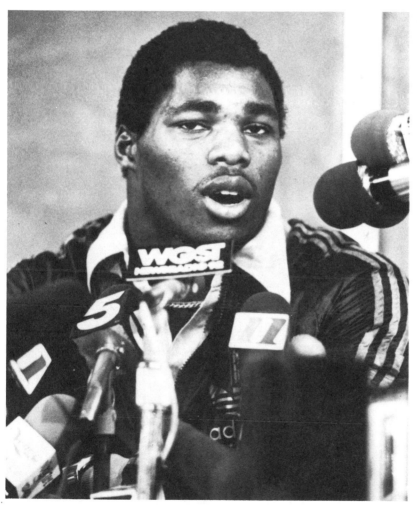

As a freshman, playing football was more than practice and games. It meant talking to newspaper and TV reporters.

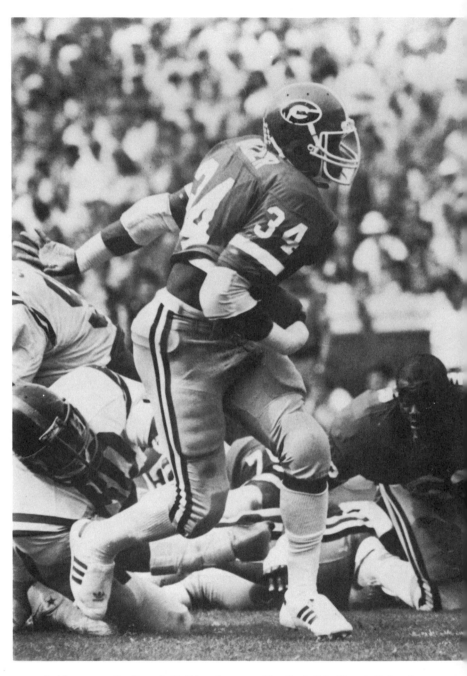

In big games, the Georgia Bulldogs began putting the ball in Herschel's hands more and more.

In the third period, Herschel scored a touchdown on two smashes into the line that covered four yards. That made the score 35-0.

Soon afterward A&M punted to the Georgia 12-yard line. And then it was all Herschel. He busted into the line for four yards, then three yards, and again for seven yards and a first down. Once more Herschel took the handoff and turned up the power. He shot ahead and outran everybody. It was 76 yards for the TD. The run gave him a total of 145 yards for the game. Coach Dooley did not believe in running up the score. He took the regulars out and let the subs finish the game. The final score was 42-0.

The next game, against Clemson, was close to the very end. Georgia was leading, 20-16, but Clemson had the ball, first-and-ten on the Georgia 10-yard line. There were still three minutes left on the clock, plenty of time to get another touchdown.

The Clemson quarterback dropped back to pass. Georgia linebacker Fran Ros charged in, reached up, and managed to get a hand on the ball. It wobbled away, where safety Jeff Hipp intercepted. He was put down on the Georgia 1-yard line, but the Bulldogs had the ball.

Time left—2:45. The Clemson Tigers had two timeouts left. The Bulldogs had to keep possession, and then possibly punt from deep in their own territory. Buck Belue got two hard yards on a keeper play, where the quarterback has a choice of lateraling the ball to a halfback or keeping it and running himself. Then, after a timeout had been called by the Tigers, Belue handed off to Herschel. The big running back slanted to the left, turned on steam, and lugged the ball to the 23-yard line. Georgia was out of danger. After that play, Clemson called its final timeout but Georgia kept possession and won, 20-16.

It was against Texas Christian University that Herschel received his first real football injury. In the first quarter, he broke into the secondary and raced 41 yards down the sideline. He was knocked out of bounds on the 8-yard line. He didn't get up right away. His ankle was hurt. He played no more in that game, but the Bulldogs won anyway, 34-3.

Herschel didn't play much the next game against Mississippi. He didn't have to. Teammate Carnie Norris filled in very well, gaining 150 yards. Herschel had only one big run for 25 yards, but in ten other carries he gained a mere 19 more. The undefeated Bulldogs won, 26-21.

By the time Georgia faced Vanderbilt, Herschel's ankle had healed completely. He proved that the first time he got his hands on the football. Vanderbilt kicked off and the Bulldogs returned the ball to their own 38-yard line. In the first two plays they gained barely two yards. But Belue gave the ball to Herschel on the next play. The tailback found a big hole in the line, broke away from the linebackers, ran past the secondary, and went all the way to the goal line — 60 yards for the touchdown.

Just minutes later, Georgia had the ball back, and Herschel was at it again. First a 38-yard gain, then 12 more. In three carries, he had already gained a total of 110 yards. By halftime, he had carried fifteen times for 207 yards.

The game wasn't really much of a contest, but it was a great one for Herschel. Though he came out early in the fourth quarter, he already had 283 yards in 23 carries, an average of 12.3 per carry. Vanderbilt coach George MacIntyre said: "Walker is the best back around. He's the difference in the football team. You can slow him down, but you can't stop him. Heck, you've got to hit him with six guys just to bring him down."

Georgia's victories mounted up. The Bulldogs defeated

Coach Dooley had never had a player like Herschel before.

Kentucky, South Carolina, and scored a tough come-from-behind victory over Florida. Then they beat Auburn, 31-21, to win the Southeast Conference championship. A final victory over their traditional rival Georgia Tech brought Georgia an undefeated season.

The game against Tech brought new glory to Herschel. Before the kickoff, he needed only 41 yards to break the national record for freshman rushers. That mark of 1,586 yards was set by the great Tony Dorsett at the University of Pittsburgh in 1973. Herschel got the yards—plus a few more. He scored touchdowns on runs of 65 and 23 yards, then added another TD on a 1-yard plunge. In all, he gained 205 yards rushing, to finish with 1,616 yards and the record.

It was on to the Sugar Bowl against Notre Dame. Georgia had a record of 11-0, while the Fighting Irish record showed nine victories, one loss, and one tie. Therefore, a victory would give the Bulldogs the national championship of college football. Georgia was favored to win by a single point.

Notre Dame scored first, cashing in on a 50-yard field goal to make the score 3-0. On the following series of plays, it looked like Georgia would take a beating. Carrying the ball for the second time, Herschel was knocked out of bounds by a Notre Dame linebacker. He went down with a thud. When he got up, his left shoulder felt sore. It had been dislocated.

As the worried Bulldogs watched, Dr. Mulherin, the Georgia team doctor, managed to pop the shoulder back in place. Herschel moved his body around to get rid of the stiffness, then trotted back out on the field.

Herschel made his presence felt immediately. He ground out the yardage, moving ahead with four runs of seven, seven, eight, and seven yards. The Irish zeroed in on Herschel and they stopped him on his next two runs. The Bulldogs had to settle for a field goal to tie the game, 3-3.

The next kickoff proved to be lucky for Georgia. The ball was booted and two Notre Dame players got under it, each trying for it. Neither got it, and Georgia picked up the bouncing ball on the Notre Dame 1-yard line. From there, Herschel dove in to the end zone and Georgia had a 10-3 lead.

Later in the second quarter, Georgia recovered another fumble on the Irish 22. Herschel ran a sweep to the right, and he scored again. Georgia now had a 17-3 lead.

Herschel had carried the Bulldogs in the first half. While the other Bulldogs had no good statistics to show, Herschel had already gained 97 yards.

Notre Dame got a touchdown in the final seconds of the third quarter and made the score 17-10. But the Bulldogs, helped by the steady play of Herschel, held on to win, 17-10. Herschel gained 150 yards and was voted the best player of the game. He had already been named to all the All-America teams.

However, he did not win the Heisman Trophy, which is given to the best football player in the country. Some said he deserved it. But George Rogers of South Carolina was first in the voting, and Hugh Green of Pittsburgh was second. Still, Herschel came in third, and no freshman had ever finished that high.

Meanwhile, back home in Wrightsville, people were cheering for Herschel Walker once again.

Chapter 5

Herschel's football success at Georgia brought him many offers which could mean big money. One group of businessmen wanted to start him off in his own insurance company. The Canadian Football League wanted him to quit school and turn professional. Herschel did not accept either offer.

The National Collegiate Athletic Association (NCAA) declared that the insurance company plan would cost him his amateur standing.

Herschel's mother put her foot down on both ideas. "You're too young," she said. "It's a big world out there. People are older and more experienced. Stay in school."

Herschel agreed. He told reporters: "I was born in this country. It doesn't seem right to leave the country just to play football." In fact, Herschel did leave the country. But it was only for a short time, and it was for track and field, not football.

Herschel loved track events, even more than football. In the spring of 1981, while he was still a freshman, he qualified for the NCAA indoor and outdoor championships in the sprints. After competing in those meets as well as some of the top meets around the country, he earned an invitation to run in Europe. In one of those meets, he had his best personal time in the 100-meter dash: 10.19 seconds. His powerful legs pumped like pistons as he covered the ground. Herschel, however, did not win many of those races. But he was competing against the best in the world and he was not embarrassing himself. He liked many sports. He played basketball, and he even took up karate.

Herschel was now a public figure, known to sports fans everywhere. And his fans wanted to know more about him, personally.

He was asked many questions:

"Do you have trouble buying clothes that fit?"

Herschel's answer: "Yes. I have a small waist, big legs, and broad shoulders. If the pants fit my legs, they have to be taken in about ten inches at the waist, and they look terrible. My clothes have to be tailor-made. That's expensive. I don't have time to have a job. I feel guilty about asking my folks for money, so I don't have many clothes."

Another question:

"What kind of music do you like?"

His answer: "Disco. I like to dance. I like music that gets me moving."

And another question:

"You're a big guy. Do you eat a lot?"

His answer: "No. I love cheeseburgers. I've cut down on candy bars, but I still eat some. And I don't seem to gain much weight."

Georgia football fans expected a lot from their favorite player, and Herschel did not disappoint them in his sophomore season of 1981. True, it was not an undefeated team. But, once again, Herschel set records. In every game he racked up more than 100 yards rushing. Against Mississippi, he gained 265; against Florida, 192; against Georgia Tech, 225. For the season, he gained a total of 1,897 yards.

The Bulldogs' only loss was to Clemson. Georgia simply played a sloppy game. In the first half, the Bulldogs fumbled four times and were intercepted twice. In the second half there were three more interceptions. Clemson took advantage of the turnovers and won, 13-3.

Many smart people thought Herschel had a good chance at the Heisman Trophy in 1981. But it was not to be. The award went to Marcus Allen, a super running back from Southern Cal. Herschel finished second, ahead of such stars as quarterback Jim McMahon of Brigham Young and Dan Marino of Pittsburgh. It was the first time a sophomore had finished so high in the voting since 1944, when Glenn Davis of West Point was also second.

The Georgia win-loss record was good enough for another invitation to the Sugar Bowl. Georgia's opponent was Pittsburgh. The Pitt Panthers had Dan Marino, one of the finest quarterbacks in college football and an excellent passer. It was a tough game all the way. Pittsburgh pulled it out in the final seconds of play, 24-20. Herschel was dogged by the Pittsburgh defense. He gained 84 yards, good for an average player but not good for him. Except for that defeat, it had been a good season.

A lot of people seemed to forget that there was another star named Walker attending Georgia. That person was Veronica Walker, Herschel's sister. She was a star on the track team. In 1982, she won All-America honors in the 100-meter dash and 400-meter relay. Maybe she couldn't beat her brother anymore, but Veronica could certainly outrun other women.

Another young lady who ran track at Georgia was Cindy

DeAngelis. Cindy and Veronica became good friends. Soon Cindy and Herschel became good friends, too. One day they would be married.

Other interesting things were beginning to happen in Herschel's life. First, there were rumors of another pro football league about to be formed. This league would play during the spring and summer months. The owners did not want competition from the National Football League (NFL). Everybody was interested in getting Herschel some day, but the new league did not care if he played another year of college football.

The NFL, meanwhile, had an old rule that stated that a player could not enter the league until his four years of college were used up. A player could claim "hardship" and ask to be drafted under extreme conditions, but Herschel did not fit into that category.

For Herschel, the 1982 season — his junior year — almost came to an end before the first kickoff. During practice, his thumb was broken. He had an operation and his hand was put in a cast.

Surprisingly, Herschel did play in the opener against Clemson. But he didn't play often and he didn't play well. He gained only 20 yards in 11 carries. However, Georgia still won.

Against Brigham Young University, Herschel was back on track. He carried the ball 31 times for 124 yards. He didn't stop for the rest of the season. He ground out 215 yards against Mississippi State, 219 against Memphis State, and 219 again against Florida. He ended the regular season with 1,752 yards rushing, almost the same as his sophomore year.

More importantly, the Bulldogs were undefeated again. In fact, they were rated as the top team in the nation.

The Heisman Trophy is awarded before the bowl games,

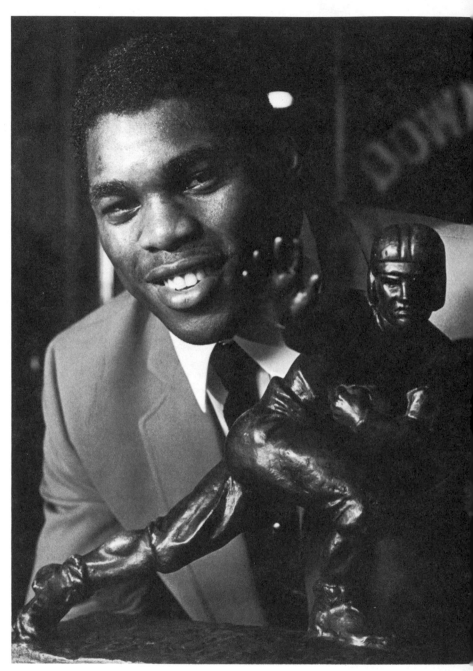

Herschel with football's grand prize, the Heisman Trophy.

and Herschel certainly was one of the top candidates. John Elway, the great quarterback from Stanford, was another. So was Eric Dickerson, the tough running back from Southern Methodist.

But the voters — who include sportswriters, sportscasters, and former Heisman winners — liked Herschel Walker the best. It was the biggest individual honor he ever won. There was one team honor to go, however, and that was the national championship.

The Georgia Bulldogs went to the Sugar Bowl one more time. Their rival in that game, Penn State, was rated the second-best team in the country. The Nittany Lions from Pennsylvania knew they had to stop Herschel to win. He carried 28 times, but was held to 103 yards, well below his normal totals. Penn State won the game, 27-23.

The records that Herschel had set in three years in college were numerous. Most of his school and Southeast Conference marks held for a long time or are still records. He gained 5,259 yards rushing in three years, and that was the third best in NCAA history. The only two players with more yards were Tony Dorsett of Pittsburgh and Charles White of Southern Cal, and those two rushers played for four years.

The broken thumb at the beginning of the season made Herschel think about his future. It was possible that he could be injured again, even more seriously. He might break an ankle or tear up a knee that could end his career. He wanted to stay in college for the full four years, but now things seemed different.

Besides, what else was there to prove? He already won the Heisman Trophy. That would be remembered in history more than any other records he could add to his already long list.

The new professional football league that would play in spring and summer had been formed. It was called the United

States Football League (USFL). One of the teams was the New Jersey Generals. It was owned by a multimillionaire named Donald Trump. Herschel decided that it wouldn't hurt to talk to Trump about turning professional. That was a mistake.

Under NCAA rules, even if Herschel did not sign a contract, he "negotiated," or talked money, with Trump. When this fact was learned, Herschel was no longer eligible to play

Herschel accepted his Heisman with much pride.

football during his senior year at Georgia. Now there was no way out. He had to turn pro. He decided to sign with Trump.

There were all sorts of rumors and stories about how much money Herschel received. Actually, it was about five and one-half million dollars for three years. His first check was for one and one-half million dollars. He gave it to his mother to deposit in the Bank of Wrightsville.

Chapter 6

When the USFL was formed, the owners knew they could never take many fans away from the NFL. The NFL as well as the colleges played in the fall. The baseball playoffs and the World Series were in the fall.

The new league couldn't get a network television contract for fall-winter games. CBS-TV had almost half the NFL games, NBC-TV had almost another half, and ABC-TV had the popular Monday Night Football. The colleges and major league baseball had the networks in deals for much of the rest of the fall.

Without television the new league, the USFL could not pay the good salaries to get good players like Herschel Walker. So there was one solution: play spring and summer football. The USFL found someone who liked the idea. That was ABC-TV.

Herschel reported to the New Jersey Generals while there was still snow on the ground. He got his old jersey number 34. In March, 1983, Herschel and the Generals took the field

Herschel gets set for a new challenge in a new uniform, that of the Generals.

against the Los Angeles Express. About 34,000 fans showed up for the game, and millions of others watched on television.

But Herschel did not do well. He did score a touchdown, but he gained only 65 yards on 18 carries. Part of the reason was that his one-time Georgia teammate Meat Cleaver Weaver, played for the Express. After the game, which the Generals lost, Cleaver said: "I never had the chance to tackle a millionaire before." Cleaver and the entire Express line ganged up on Herschel.

Herschel said later: "It's a lot tougher out there than I thought it would be. A lot of guys had more speed than I expected to see."

Herschel did not mention that he had only one week of practice with the Generals. His line of Generals hadn't had much practice, either, so it was not as coordinated as Herschel had been used to at Georgia. But Herschel refused to offer alibis. He was getting paid a lot of money to run with the football, not to make excuses.

His second pro game was not better. He gained only 60 yards on 13 carries. He also fumbled twice. In the next game, which was the home opener at Giants Stadium in New Jersey, Herschel and the Generals heard a lot of boos as they lost a third straight game. Herschel managed only 39 yards in 19 carries. It may have been the worst game of his life.

"I don't know what I'm doing right or wrong," he said after the game. "I'm still learning. In this league, football is a lot different from college."

One all-star running back, Walter Payton, the future Hall of Fame back with the Chicago Bears, had seen Herschel play. His advice: "Maybe the offensive line has heard so much about Herschel, they think he can do it on his own. My advice to him is, keep your head up and don't let a few bad games get you down."

The NFL coaches didn't think highly of the new league. Chuck Noll, the head coach of the Pittsburgh Steelers whose team won four Super Bowls, said: "Really, it's just minor league football." He admitted that there were a number of good players scattered around the league. However, he said, the teams as a whole were a sorry lot.

Suddenly, though, things changed around for Herschel. He became one of those good players. First, on March 31, 1983, he and Cindy were married. A few nights later, he scored three touchdowns and gained 177 yards against the Arizona Wranglers. After that, the 100-yard-plus games became common. He found his groove.

He reached his peak against the Denver Gold. In that game, he became the first USFL player to gain more than 1,000 yards rushing in one season. And he topped off his performance with an 80-yard run, his longest since high school.

Herschel hated to lose games and the Generals had trouble winning. That first season they won six and lost twelve. Herschel did lead the league in rushing with 1,812. That was pretty good after the slow start.

He also led the league in making money. In addition to his big salary, he earned extra money — called endorsements — by letting big companies use his name to sell products.

But he earned his money in 1983. Remember, he had just played a full college schedule the fall before, then played in a bowl game, then played 18 games with the Generals. He had played in 10 of the previous 12 months. Here was a guy who was glad to take, or peel, off the number 34 jersey and put it away for a while.

But he did not rest completely. He went back to the University of Georgia to earn his diploma and a degree in criminal justice.

When Herschel returned to the Generals for the 1984 season, other college stars had also joined the USFL. One was a quarterback, Steve Young. He signed with the Los Angeles Express for a multimillion dollar contract. Donald Trump wanted to make certain that Herschel was happy, so he signed Herschel to a bigger contract. And what a contract it was!

Herschel would be guaranteed two million dollars a year

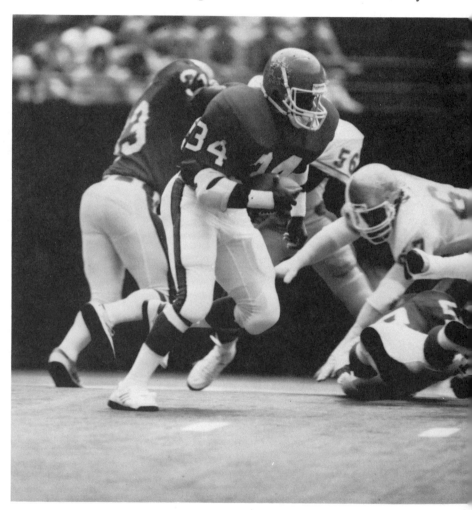

The USFL would soon die, but not without the fabulous records of Herschel Walker to remember.

through the 1989 season. If he got hurt, he would still get paid. If the USFL went out of business, he would still get paid. And if Herschel got drafted by a team from the other league, the NFL, Trump would continue to pay him in full.

Or, if Herschel wanted, he could get his money over a period of years, assuring him of being a rich man even after he got out of football. Over all, he could get more than thirty-four million dollars over the next thirty-seven years. Almost one million dollars a year. The money was fine — more than fine. But the 1984 season was a rough one for Herschel. He was glad he had the big contract.

He hurt his right shoulder. He had to be careful how he was tackled, how he ran, and how he fell to the ground. Again, he got off to a slow start. But as the season wore on, he picked up steam. At the end of the year, he was third in the league with 1,339 yards gained rushing. He also had 16 touchdowns. The Generals improved, too. They won fourteen games and lost only four, even though the league was getting better.

In 1985, Herschel had an amazing season. He ran for 2,411 yards on 438 attempts. He scored 21 touchdowns on the ground and another on a pass play. The professional football writers for the league voted him the Most Valuable Player title — best player in the league.

Things were looking good for Herschel, but not good for the league in 1985. Fans were not coming out to see games. Television viewers didn't seem to want to watch football in the spring and summer. Football fans were used to the fall and early winter playoffs, like they had in the NFL. The USFL announced that it would have to try a new schedule to compete with the NFL. It wouldn't be easy.

Most experts were sure it wouldn't be easy. In fact, they were almost sure it was impossible. The Dallas Cowboys of the NFL were among those who didn't think the USFL would last. Therefore, when they had their fifth-round draft choice in the spring of 1985, they chose Herschel Walker. It was a strange idea to take a pro player in the draft instead of a college star. It was a gamble, but a gamble that paid off. The USFL went out of business soon after. Many of the best players, such as Steve Young, Kelvin Bryant, and others, moved to the NFL.

It was a peculiar situation for Herschel Walker. He was the one single football player who helped make the USFL popular. But something was more unusual. In college, he spent most of his time chasing the records of Tony Dorsett of the University of Pittsburgh. Now Dorsett played for the Cowboys and would be Herschel's teammate.

Was there room enough for two great running backs on the same team? Would they be jealous of each other? Only time would tell.

Chapter 7

Herschel Walker's new contract with the Dallas Cowboys would pay him a million dollars a year for five years, beginning in 1986. That is when he would join the Cowboys. He would also receive all the money due to him from Donald Trump and the New Jersey Generals. Football had made Herschel a very rich young man.

"You could retire on the money Donald Trump owes you," a reporter said to him. "Why do you keep playing football?"

"I don't need to play," replied Herschel. "I WANT to play. I love to play football."

The reporter asked another question: "Are you trying to prove you can play football in the NFL?"

Herschel never lost his poise. "I'm not trying to prove anything," he said. "Just remember this, they said I couldn't play at Georgia because I came from a small high school. I think I played well. Then they said I couldn't play in the USFL. I played well. They said I couldn't catch the ball. I had 80 catches with the Generals. They said the USFL wasn't

Herschel caught 76 passes in his first season with the Cowboys. This was a team record.

much of a league. Those guys were all pro football players. Now, let's wait and see if I can play in the NFL."

The big question, however, was how Herschel would get along with Tony Dorsett, with two great players sharing or fighting for one position. Would Dorsett be upset because of Herschel's big contract after all that Dorsett had done for the Cowboys for much less money? Dorsett answered that question himself.

He was about to play his tenth season with the Cowboys, yet he was receiving far less money than Herschel, as everyone knew. Dorsett said, "If you want unity on a team, then everybody has to be treated as equals." But Dorsett was quick to point out that no one was mad at Herschel because of the big contract. "If he can get more money, more power to him," said Tony.

When Dorsett was asked if he and Herschel would play in the backfield at the same time, he shrugged.

"I can't see it," he said. "Sure, I can block. So can Walker. But we're getting paid to run with the ball, not block for each other."

Before Herschel could run with the ball, he had to learn the Cowboys' system. All football teams use different systems, including blocking assignments and pass routes. A quarterback might call plays himself in the huddle or use a play sent in by the coach. The coaches built their systems on the types of players they had on the team. For example, a tailback might run better to his right than to his left. A running back might be a good pass receiver, or he might be just fair.

As Herschel watched from the sidelines, he realized how much he would miss the man who blocked for him on the Generals, Maurice Carthon. Carthon, a star from Arkansas State, had signed with the New York Giants. Herschel thought he was as good as they come.

By the time Dallas played the Giants in the first game of the 1986 season, Herschel knew most of the Cowboys' system. But he wasn't always sure of himself. Still, the fans were glad to have him and they cheered for him and wanted to like him. A few times, he lined up in the wrong place, but the fans were quick to forgive him. They certainly did not boo him. When Herschel fumbled on the Dallas 14-yard line, and the Giants recovered and scored a touchdown, the fans just waited. They knew that the newcomer would come through for them, sooner or later.

Tony Dorsett was still considered the first-team tailback, but he injured his ankle in the first half and had to sit on the bench the rest of the game.

Herschel excelled in the second half. With 2:10 left to play, the Cowboys trailed the Giants, 28-24. They had the ball on their own 28-yard line. The goal line seemed to be a mile away.

On the first play, Dallas quarterback Danny White passed to Herschel. The big back broke four arm tackles and was off to a 23-yard gain. A screen pass to Herschel lost two yards. Then White hit Tony Hill with a pass that was good for 35 yards. The Cowboys kept grinding out the yards until they reached the Giants 10-yard line. Only 50 seconds remained on the clock. It was third down, four yards to go.

Because they were behind by four points, the Cowboys needed a touchdown. A three-point field goal would not be enough.

Dallas lined up in a shotgun formation, where the quarterback lines up a few yards behind the center instead of right behind him. That seemed to indicate a pass was coming up. But it turned out to be a trap play, with Herschel carrying the ball up the middle. Gary Reasons, the Giants' inside

linebacker, got a hand on Herschel, but Herschel shook free
and stormed into the end zone for the winning touchdown.

One player cannot turn a team into Super Bowl
champions. The Dallas Cowboys once had enough good
players to go to several Super Bowls and even win a couple.
But many of their best players had grown old and retired. The

Herschel finally became the Cowboys' key running back.

team had to rebuild. Herschel Walker was a step in that direction in 1986.

Yet there were times when the Cowboys almost reached their old glory, and they had the satisfaction of knocking a rival team out of the playoffs. The next season, 1987, for example, the Cowboys beat the Los Angeles Rams in the next-to-last game to knock them out of post-season playoffs.

A week later, the Cowboys did the same thing to the St. Louis Cardinals. In the game against the Cardinals, Herschel rushed for 137 yards and caught three passes for 50 more yards.

But, most important of all was the winning touchdown against the Cardinals. On that play, Herschel did not touch the ball at all. The Cowboys lined up in a formation they had used earlier in the game. The Cardinals recognized the formation. It called for a handoff to Herschel. The Cardinals shifted over to meet the tailback coming through the line.

But it was a fake. Dallas quarterback Steve Pelluer kept the ball. Almost the entire Cardinal team chased Herschel, who pretended to have the ball. Pelluer took off in the opposite direction. Nobody was near him as he scored. The final score was 21-16, Dallas. So in a way, Herschel helped the team get all of its touchdowns.

With Herschel getting all the headlines, the Dallas front office decided to keep Tony Dorsett happy. They felt they owed the veteran something for his long and faithful service. They gave in to his wish to be traded. Tony went to the Denver Broncos before the start of the 1988 season. Herschel remained as the Cowboys' number one tailback.

With his new-found money and new-found confidence, Herschel did not forget where he came from. He presented his family with a new, big ranch-style home.

The 1988 season was not a happy one for the Dallas Cowboys and their fans. The team had its worst season since its very first one, almost three decades before.

But Herschel, the once chubby youngster, did not quit. In 1988, he was a 1,000-yard rusher. In fact, his 1,514 yards ranked second in the NFL. He also had developed into a fine pass receiver. He caught 53 passes for 505 yards. His combined receiving and rushing yardage ranked third in the league.

His statistics and his good play impressed everybody, in and out of Dallas. When the 1988 season was over, coaches and players voted Herschel to be the starting halfback for the National Football Conference in the Pro Bowl. That made him as good, if not better, than any halfback in the league.

But as the 1989 season unfolded, not all was well with the Cowboys, and it began affecting Herschel, too. The team got a new owner before the start of the season, and the new owner brought in his own coach to replace Tom Landry. Landry had been the only coach the Cowboys ever had in nearly 30 years. The new coach had a new system, and it didn't work. The Cowboys lost their first five games. In four of those games, they weren't even close.

Herschel kept plugging away, giving a good effort for a team going bad. It wasn't good enough to save the Cowboys, though, and the Cowboy fans were getting impatient with the new owner and the new coach, Jimmy Johnson.

Meanwhile, the Minnesota Vikings, with a much better team, were struggling. Their record was 3 victories and 2 losses in what had hoped to be a promising season. One of the Vikings' biggest problems: they needed a first-class running back. And what team can pick up a great runner in the middle of the season? It seemed impossible.

Well, the impossible came true. The Cowboys, desperate to change their fate, traded Herschel to the

Vikings on October 12, 1989, in a trade that stunned football followers across the country.

As good as Herschel was and as much as he could help the Vikings, the trade received mixed feelings in Minnesota. Some fans were joyous with the prospect of getting him. Others said the Vikings paid too dearly with the players they gave up and with draft choices.

The trade was made in the middle of the week, and Herschel had only a few hours to work out with his new team before a big game against Central Division rival Green Bay. But the Viking players, hungry for a playoff spot, were glad to have him in their offense. Plus he had no trouble fitting in with the team.

In his first game, Herschel began grinding his way through the Packer defense. Before the day was over, the Vikings won with ease, 26-14, and Herschel finished with 148 yards. It not only was a great game under the conditions, it was one of the best games of his career.

After that, the Vikings began turning more and more to Herschel. Maybe too much. Though it was midseason, the Vikings began building their offense around their new found star. But nobody gains 148 yards every game, not even Herschel. The team struggled but made the playoffs by winning the division. Herschel finished with a good year—915 yards rushing and 423 more on receptions. Not great for him, but good enough for the Vikings to begin planning ahead to build their attack around his abilities. In fact, the team made some changes in the offseason to bring in assistant coaches in better tune with the running game.

"Herschel is only 27 years old," said the team's general manager, Mike Lynn, who made the trade. "Hopefully, he'll be here to help us another three to five years."

Herschel was satisfied with the Vikings, too. He had a

contract that was worth a million dollars a year through 1991. The trade sparked more interest in him and that helped his endorsements, which were worth more money than his football contracts.

"I enjoy playing here," he said at the end of the season. "This team has a lot of talent."

And the Vikings felt likewise. After all, Herschel has a lot of talent, too.

The Vikings paid a big price to acquire Herschel.

CAREER STATISTICS

YEAR	CLUB	RUSHING				PASS RECEIVING			
		# of CARRIES	TOTAL YARDS	AVG. YARDS	TOUCH-DOWNS	PASSES CAUGHT	TOTAL YARDS	AVG. YARDS	TOUC DOW
1980	Georgia	274	1,616	5.9	15	7	70	10.0	
1981	Georgia	385	1,891	4.9	18	14	84	6.0	
1982	Georgia	335	1,752	5.2	16	5	89	17.8	
1983	Generals	412	1,812	4.4	17	53	489	9.2	
1984	Generals	293	1,339	4.6	16	40	528	13.2	
1985	Generals	438	2,411	5.5	21	37	467	12.6	
1986	Ccwboys	151	737	4.9	12	76	837	11.0	
1987	Cowboys	209	891	4.3	7	60	715	11.9	
1988	Cowboys	361	1,514	4.2	5	53	505	9.5	
1989	Cowboys & Vikings	250	915	3.7	7	40	423	10.6	
1990	Vikings	184	770	4.2	5	35	315	9.0	

Index